IMPACTFUL DEVELOPMENT

IMPACTFUL DEVELOPMENT

Growing Your Business While Making a Difference

How to Profit with Purpose Through Residential Real Estate Development

MICHAEL J. ROKOSKI

Michael J. Rokoski
support@impactful-development.com
www.impactful-development.com/copyright

Impactful Development, Michael J. Rokoski —1st ed.

DEDICATION

This book is dedicated to all the hard-working people out there trying to do the right thing, take care of their families, live the American Dream, buy a house, and live a simple but great life. To my parents, who at 16 and 19 raised me and my brother and made us feel so special and taken care of. To my daughter, Shelby, it has been the greatest joy to be your dad and so special to watch the amazing human you are and the lady you are becoming!

CONTENTS

Introduction

Growing Your Real Estate Business

As a real estate professional, you understand that housing is one of the most prominent problems our country faces. Your passion for finding people homes that enrich their lives got you into this business, but today's landscape makes increasing your revenue mentally exhausting and challenging.

The traditional way a real estate broker tries to find listings and buyers doesn't work as well as you need. You need a way to **create your own inventory**, to be seen as a valuable asset versus a cost, and to establish controllable real growth for your business.

Your Opportunity to Create Impact

You've probably overlooked one of the biggest opportunities right in front of you. This opportunity will enable you to diversify and create a more significant revenue pipeline for you and your team. Building wealth through real estate by adding land development to your business isn't as difficult as you may think.

In this book, I'll take you through the whole real estate development process and show you how simple it is to make a new revenue pipeline without borrowing millions of dollars or sacrificing your family's future with big gambles.

As a real estate developer, your impact reaches out into your community—to the country. A person can find work but can't find a house they can afford. Different studies say we need to build 1.4 to 1.8 million housing units every year in the U.S. to keep up, and it may be more than that now. My goal with reaching out to real estate professionals like you is to show people across the nation how they can help alleviate that problem over the next ten years.

With Impactful Development, you build more wealth into your business, gain more control over how you conduct your business, and love your work more. You will be able to capitalize on investing in ways you hadn't thought of before **while creating massive impact**.

This Book Contains Your Future

Books changed my life and led me on a more productive, impactful path to success and wealth. In this book, I share the strategies I learned over the past 20-plus years in real estate that enabled me to go from nothing to $100 million plus a year with a small team of six people.

It takes some strategy, but more importantly, changing your mindset! This book will help engage you to see the opportunities that you didn't realize were right in front of you the whole time. More than that, it takes what I call a DTFW™ mindset, which I'll explain later. This one action alone will help ensure you don't make the biggest costly mistake that many real estate professionals make today.

What if I could reveal how to build another pipeline for your business just by showing you how to recognize the opportunities right in front of you?

You don't have to keep working long hours managing listings and buyers. You don't have to feel exhausted trying to keep up. Read this book and let me know how you feel about your business's future after you finish it.

CHAPTER 1

The Affordable Housing Challenge

It is a Big Problem, but There is a Solution

We're not keeping up.

Across the United States, the demand for homes increases faster than we can build them. Adding to this overall issue, the housing that is being built isn't at the affordable price point of those who need it, such as the middle class. This gap in our housing industry is making an already negative impact even worse. When a family cannot afford a home, it limits their opportunities to earn more and causes slower GDP growth.

> The American economy loses about $2 trillion a year in lower wages and productivity due to the shortage in affordable housing. Affordable housing boosts local economies and supports job creation and retention.[1]

[1] *The problem.* National Low Income Housing Coalition. (n.d.). https://nlihc.org/explore-issues/why-we-care

This shortage is expected to get worse as millennials and Gen Zers enter the homebuying field for family homes. America is short approximately 3.2 million homes, but construction is not keeping up with the growing demand to close that gap.[2] We must triple construction efforts to close the existing 3.5 million home gap in 2-3 years.

This broad housing shortage goes back decades, affecting multiple regions and sectors. The affordable houses that our middle-class families need make up a huge part of that gap.

We need to build a minimum of 1.4 million housing units annually to keep up with the expected population growth over the next ten years. Some studies say we need even more than that, such as Rosen Consulting Group's report, which states we need more than 2 million housing units per year.[3] Add to that, we've had an influx of people for other reasons such as immigration since those studies were done. You can see how the need for affordable and workforce housing keeps increasing.

Housing hurdles for the middle-class family.

Why is it that people can work hard, have good credit, and still not be able to own a home? It's due to the overall housing shortage in the United States. A blue-collar, middle-class

---

2 Sparber, S. (2023, December 16). *Why houses are so expensive, explained in one chart.* Axios.com. https://www.axios.com/2023/12/16/housing-market-why-homes-expensive-chart-inventory

3 Rosen, K. T., Bank, D., Hall, M., Reed, S., & Goldman, C. (2021, June). Social and economic benefits of building more housing. www.nar.realtor. https://www.nar.realtor/sites/default/files/documents/Housing-is-Critical-Infrastructure-Social-and-Economic-Benefits-of-Building-More-Housing-6-15-2021.pdf

worker has a family and can't find affordable housing, so what happens? They live with their parents or families, which can lead to a toxic situation for everyone. Or, they rent a house, apartment, or trailer because they can't enjoy the financial and emotional benefits of homeownership.

> In 2023, homeownership was cited by 74% of U.S. adults as being part of the American dream. Affordability is a major obstacle for 73% of those wanting to own a home.[4]

This is a real problem, but often, even in areas where new housing is going, it doesn't solve the problems for the middle-class family. The majority of newly-built housing is not affordable.[5] Think about the people around you. You know someone who is being impacted by this situation today. When you open your eyes, you will see that we not only need to boost our housing supply, but we need to build more homes priced in the range that families can afford.[6]

There is a solution.

We can be part of the solution and provide affordable housing to blue-collar homebuyers and retirees by focusing on

---

[4] Ostrowski, J. (2023, April 19). 73% of aspiring homeowners cite affordability as their primary obstacle. Bankrate. https://www.bankrate.com/mortgages/homeownership-remains-centerpiece-of-american-dream/

[5] Sparber, S. (2023, December 16). Why houses are so expensive, explained in one chart. Axios.com. https://www.axios.com/2023/12/16/housing-market-why-homes-expensive-chart-inventory

[6] Tracey, M. D. (2023, June 8). *Study: Middle-income buyers suffer most in housing shortage.* www.nar.realtor. https://www.nar.realtor/magazine/real-estate-news/study-middle-income-buyers-suffer-most-in-housing-shortage

single-family units and townhouses. With a passion for building up our communities through impacting individuals who need our help the most, real estate developers and professionals can make a difference. This book takes you through a process that allows you to maintain control to ensure your efforts help those who need it.

The top five builders in the United States built 227,105 homes in 2023[7], primarily single-family units. By building a relationship with builders, the door is open for you to create a huge impact on our housing industry. With a work-hard attitude focused on being thorough, efficient, and diligent, you'll help builders overcome the issues inflation and supply disruptions have caused.

...and it's not that complex.

Don't get overwhelmed by overthinking what a developer is, what a developer does, and how you can create an additional revenue stream for yourself by doing something good. You can diversify your income and create a bigger pipeline for you and your team if you're in real estate already. You're going to be able to make a positive impact on the communities you love.

This book will dive into each aspect of the process and show you how simple it can be. It doesn't have to involve borrowing millions of dollars and taking big gambles. It simply takes your willingness to adopt a proven process that lets you pick

---

[7] *2024 - builder 100.* Builder . (n.d.). https://www.builderonline.com/builder-100/builder-100-list/2024

up the torch to help solve the affordable housing problem in your local market.

Why Real Estate?

I grew up with a mom who became pregnant when she was 15 and gave birth to me at the young age of 16. My dad was 19 years old and became a truck driver. They worked hard, but we bounced from home to home while they tried to secure better job positions. My parents never owned a home, moving from one rental to another.

When I was 12 or 13 years old, I decided I wanted more out of life. Books got me through that phase and changed my life. I read books like *Think and Grow Rich* by Napoleon Hill and some of the first books published by Tony Robbins. My entire mindset on the future changed, and I learned about the challenges of affordable housing after school.

Remembering what it was like to move between 8 and 10 homes as a child impacted my career in the mortgage, real estate, and development business beyond high school. My parents provided me with a loving home that allowed me to adapt to our frequent moves. I also saw the negative impact this exact situation had on the "new kids," who didn't have that strong family structure. They couldn't make friends and didn't do as well in school. Many times, they were sad, depressed, and insecure.

Beginning to make a difference.

When I first entered the mortgage business, I specialized in first-time home buyer lending and 100% financing. I have thousands of cases where we helped someone with only $500-$1000 to their name get into homeownership during that time. I've been blessed to be part of the movement helping someone's family member, friend, or neighbor's son or daughter overcome the challenge of being able to afford a home. My business continues to make a positive change to overcome the gap in our affordable housing.

The Power of Homeownership™

The Federal Reserve did a study showing interesting results about people who owned a home versus those who spent their life renting. The study discovered that the average worth of someone over the age of 65 who had owned their home was 45 times greater than someone who had rented their entire life.[8]

> The average worth of someone over the age of 65 who had owned their home was 45 times greater than someone who had rented their entire life.

A generational mindset with homeownership influences how people think of where they live when they grow up. My parents owned a home, so I should also own one. My parents always rented, so I probably should just rent. When you change your mindset from settling for renting to seeking out

[8] https://www.federalreserve.gov/publications/2023-economic-well-being-of-us-households-in-2022-housing.htm

homeownership, you help your children and future generations of your family.

It's more than the money—it goes beyond that. Children within a family-owned home suffer less depression and anxiety. They tend to have better grades in school. Businesses tend to retain employees who own homes better than renters, providing more stability for those children. Employers see a homeowner as a more stable individual they can count on, and sometimes, that helps build more trust between them that carries over into a more stable home environment.

Improving the local housing affordability issues boosts the community. When families own their homes, they set down roots and become more active in the community. Bonds of friendship and alliances that contribute to the area's economic well-being are made. The local area becomes more attractive to potential residents, keeping real estate agents busier.[9]

Build-to-Rent Impacts Supply

Blackstone Inc. figured out how to scale the management and ownership of single-family homes. The company already has a massive portfolio of single-family homes, and they announced a deal to acquire a build-to-rent landlord, Tricon Residential

---

9 *Research series: How does homeownership contribute to social and civic engagement?*. Habitat for Humanity. (n.d.). https://www.habitat.org/our-work/impact/research-series-how-does-homeownership-contribute-to-social-and-civic-engagement#:~:text=Supporting%20residential%20stability%20increases%20social,better%20physical%20and%20mental%20health.

Inc.[10] (These landlords can be referred to as BTR and BFR or Build-to-Rent and Build-For-Rent respectively.)

These communities would have been single-family and townhome communities that sold the homes, but they're now entirely off the market because they're being rented and not sold. Blackstone is just one company that's taken housing opportunities off the market for a buyer—for a new family or young couple wanting to own a home. Just this one deal involves 38,000 homes that cannot be sold, and there are more deals like this out there.

Blackstone's new acquisition is not evil, nor is this business model! BTR is providing an alternative to apartments, but they are causing an issue with closing the homeownership gap. They come with the downside of how the loss of so many homes on the market impacts the "supply" of available opportunities. This book is built around how to offset this FOR SALE builders and help provide a solution to our country's homeownership challenges.

We Need Passionate Developers

The housing problem is very real. Without the help of people passionate about affordable and workforce housing who wish to do good while making money at it, it's going to keep getting worse. Is it possible to add another revenue stream to your

---

[10] Clark, P. (2024, January 19). *Blackstone is buying landlord Tricon Private for $3.5 billion.* Bloomberg.com. https://www.bloomberg.com/news/articles/2024-01-19/blackstone-is-buying-landlord-tricon-private-for-3-5-billion

existing real estate business while doing good? Can anyone establish a development business to correct this problem in their community? Yes. Keep reading to find out how.

CHAPTER 2

Real Estate Professionals: Create Your Own Inventory™

Is This Your Reality?

You spend your days prospecting by scrolling through Zillow listings and paying for leads. Your money and time revolve around building your "name recognition" through postcard mailings, billboard advertising, and marketing campaigns. You are partnering with lenders and taking the right steps to get your name in front of buyers and sellers.

Each day keeps you moving between meeting people for showings, negotiations, organizing signage, managing repairs, and everything else. You are on top of all those things to ensure you are the one they call when it's time to list their home. You have mastered techniques to find the sweet spot between what they want to list their home for and what it's actually worth.

It's a challenge to cultivate your sphere of influence to get referrals, and you're doing all the above to keep it strong. You continually reinvest in it as you should.

Would you like to enhance the work you do now and create your own inventory?

What if I could show you a way to enhance the work you do now and create your own inventory? Stay with me on this, and I'll show you how you can bring in more money while maintaining control throughout the process.

Do Your Clients Look at You as an Expense or an Asset?

A successful real estate business is very rewarding, but the traditional way sometimes becomes mentally exhausting. Sellers often want unrealistic prices for their properties, and they want you to work for cheap. Buyers aren't always truthful about their situation.

You give up time and gas money showing properties to buyers, all the while hoping they're qualified. You hope they don't quit their job or buy a new car before the sale closes. You hope they're honest about what they can afford when many times they are not.

To protect yourself, you must have a good mortgage partner, attorney, and insurance partner in place. You attempt to make sure the buyer is pre-qualified, that they understand the process, and that you are making the right disclosures to cover yourself.

When you find a seller, they often argue that their home is worth more than it is on the marketplace. You must convince them of their home's true worth and what it can realistically sell for. You have to show them the psychology of listing their home—how photos, language in the listing, showings, negotiations, and inspections play a part in selling their home.

Closing deals means diving deeper into psychology. You are called upon during the nighttime hours. You are often expected to spend weekends showing houses. You end up playing the marriage counselor or feeling like a part-time babysitter when the kids are at the viewing.

Your name recognition gets you the calls. Then, after the call, you hustle to keep the client doing all of the above. In the end, you are pushed to list for the highest selling price while being expected to work for the cheapest rate and spend the most on marketing.

Land Doesn't Have Emotion™

There is another way to get sales that doesn't involve mastering this psychology of general brokerage. I'll show you a process with less emotion and less negotiation that shifts your role from being a "cost" to an "asset" to the buyer.

Why does enhancing your real estate business by becoming a developer work? Land Doesn't Have Emotion™. It doesn't care what color the walls are painted. The process works based on facts.

> The process is realistic and puts you in control.

Builder clients are generally less emotionally involved and require less psychology than traditional real estate buyers. Developing these relationships isn't as difficult as you may think. The process is realistic and puts you in control.

The Smarter Alternative

When you control the land and lots, and you put the deals together, you're an asset. The builders and clients no longer see you as a cost. You close more deals with fewer negotiations.

Everybody Sues Everyone For Everything

There's a litigious nature to traditional real estate. Everyone is looking for someone who has done them wrong to sue. Your risk as an agent is high, so you carry insurance.

It doesn't matter if you're innocent. There is always someone looking for another with deep pockets to take advantage of in real estate situations. You still need to know how to defend yourself.

Reduce lawsuit risks.

On the other hand, builders understand and welcome co-broke commissions. They realize that co-brokes help bring in more buyers, agents, and other people to move more properties.

This perspective helps you reduce the litigious nature of your efforts. Think back to whether or not your clients see you as a "cost" or an "asset." When you call your clients with the developer model, you bring them opportunities they cannot wait to discuss with you.

NAR Settlement.[11]

The simple things can cause significant issues. When you tell sellers that the commission is 6% but leave out that they can choose to save 3%, they can get rude. Perhaps you have experienced this already.

Most lawsuits happen when there is not full disclosure. In this case, it is about how much of the fee stays with the listing agent and how much goes toward the buyer's agent. Private home sellers are not very accepting of co-broke commissions.

I will show you how to create this shift in perspective and minimize your risk of litigation. If you are ready to make this transition, Chapter Three takes you through the mindset you must have to make this work. Are you ready?

[11] What the NAR Settlement Means for Home Buyers and Sellers." Nar.realtor, 2024, www.nar.realtor/the-facts/what-the-nar-settlement-means-for-home-buyers-and-sellers.

CHAPTER 3

Mindset Matters - Don't Skip This Chapter

I know you want to learn about the process, but your mindset and approach will set you up for success or failure. DON'T SKIP THIS CHAPTER.

Be a Missionary, Not a Mercenary

For this process to work, you must be a missionary entrepreneur, not a mercenary one.

> We are missionary entrepreneurs who have a passion for providing homeownership.

A missionary entrepreneur has a passion for providing homeownership. If you have a missionary mindset, you desire to provide affordable and high-quality housing at a high level that delivers value to the new owner. You have a goal that makes everyone win.

If you're a missionary entrepreneur, you are more innovative and creation-driven. You're doing what's best for everyone concerned on your team, your clients, and the end users.

Over time, you become highly valued and make more money. You sleep better at night because you go to sleep thinking about being of service to someone.

Meanwhile, a mercenary entrepreneur gets the sale no matter the cost or the people involved. It's okay to take it from someone else. They live in a scarcity mindset and look at competition differently.

The mercenary entrepreneur is driven by what they can take from someone else and how they can keep someone from taking it from them. They don't have as much long-term stability, and they usually don't experience as much peace.

Lay your foundation.

Remember, you are playing the long game! Make sure you lay your business foundation here. Do it correctly. Don't just race to get it done.

Which One Are You?

You'll succeed with a missionary mindset. You'll fail with a mercenary mindset.

If you're a mercenary entrepreneur, please close this book now. In fact, you can email me, and I will refund your purchase. I want to work with those people who have a heart to serve and grow and make money doing it.

CHAPTER 4

Redefining Becoming a Developer

The Traditional Idea

When most people think of a real estate developer, they think about what they see on CNBC or the book covers. These show massive projects like high rises, Miami Beach condos, or large high-end properties in New York City, Los Angeles, and Chicago.

> Look at what being a developer closer to home may look like.

These are all great and have their purpose, but those are not the only developer opportunities waiting to be found. I want you to shift your thoughts about real estate development outside of those large projects and imagine what being a developer closer to home may look like.

Break the seal for additional revenue.

By shifting your idea of a developer to a more simplified definition, you can see the potential that's right outside your door. A developer is simply anyone who subdivides or provides lots.

> A developer is simply anyone who subdivides or provides lots.

Imagine you find a one-acre lot, contract it for $50,000, and get it subdivided into two half-acre lots. You then contact a builder and offer both to the builder at $35,000 each. You've just made $20,000 and have two listings. You just "developed" a tract of land, and you're a developer.

You have just "broken the seal" by adding a new pipeline to your business and creating a revenue stream you had not considered before. You don't need $10 million to break the seal. That one acre is enough.

No Real Estate License Required

Don't confuse being a broker with being a developer. You don't have to be a broker to be a developer.

A broker is someone who represents other people who wish to buy or sell. They're a third party. A broker is licensed to represent others.

The developer is a principal in the transaction. They are the buyer or seller. Just like you don't need a real estate license to buy or sell your home, you don't need one to be a developer. You may want one, though.

Disclaimer: Check your local requirements for subdividing and selling lots. Minimum sizes allowed may vary, and local zoning laws may involve other requirements for developers.

Helpful Tips For Getting Started

In the illustration above, I showed you how easy it is to get started in this business on your own. However, I do have some helpful advice.

1 - Work with a broker.
A developer who is not a broker should find a broker. You want to coordinate with a broker who is a land expert, especially when you are new at this. In most states, agency requirements allow you to do this. Check with yours.

Even if you are already a broker, coordinating with a different broker can give you an advantage. A broker who specializes in land sales for your local area can increase your potential. You will be able to learn the ins and outs of this specialty for yourself and eventually not need them.

2 - Research as much as you can.

If you're astute and have done your research, you can choose to represent yourself. If you've read the Unified Development Ordinance (UDO), know your zoning map, met with the planners, and all the other steps, then this may work in your favor.

3 - Work with licensed people, even if you are not.

I know of no municipalities or states that dictate you must be licensed to be a real estate developer. Do not confuse this with utility contractors. People mistakenly consider the utility contractor the developer, but they are not the developer. You are the developer—they are contracted by the person who owns the dirt.

As the developer, you are the person who is leading the subdivision as the owner or the controlling party. You will be involved with others who need licenses, such as people who need ones for engineering, surveying, utilities, wetlands consulting, etc. As the owner or contract holder of the property, you don't need licensing.

4 - Learn as much as you can.

I have a course coming up that this book leads into. In that course, we will give you a checklist of questions to ask a broker. You'll get questions like these on that checklist.

- How much experience do you have with land?
- How long have you had your real estate license?

The tutorial will guide you through how to conduct the interview before you enter into a relationship with that broker. You'll avoid the issues that can slow you down, should you work with the wrong type of broker.

You can make this process work for you by becoming a land person. When you understand the right questions to ask and know your local market, you build a revenue pipeline that benefits your business and the community. **When you control and understand land and lots, you create more opportunities!**

You do not have to start big, but you do need to start.

At the young age of six, Warren Buffett bought multi-packs of gum and sold them per piece to earn a small return on his first investment in life. Feeding off the success, he purchased a nickel machine, repaired it with his partner, and set it up in a barbershop. After one week, they had enough to buy another pinball machine.[12]

Warren continued to expand his business by selling soft drinks and having a paper route. When he turned 14, he invested his money in 40 acres of land. He rented this land out at a profit. He never stopped building, learning, and improving his revenue stream.

"I bought a machine for $25 in 1946 and built a small empire out of it."
~ Warren Buffett

Note: 99% of Warren Buffett's net worth came after age 55!

Land Doesn't Have Emotion™

Now, we are going to start diving into our process. Remember that Land Doesn't Have Emotion™, and we are going to show you how to build another pipeline into your business.

Start by understanding the needs of your market. Does your market need townhomes? Does it need single-family homes?

[12] Schroeder, A. (2009). The Snowball: Warren Buffett and the business of life. Bantam Books.

Who are the builders fulfilling the need in that market? I help you figure this out in Chapter 5, and then we go deeper.

I'll show you how to dig into the UDO to maximize the value of the property you're considering.

- Understand the UDO (Unified Development Ordinance).
- Understand the zoning maps for your area.
- Use a large printed map that's color-coded by zoning type.

Then, in Chapter 6, I'll help you understand how to find a Good Piece Of Land™. These lots may become possible rezoning opportunities. You may come across a place zoned for commercial or industrial use, but it really shouldn't be. It would make an excellent location for a neighborhood. In many cases, the neighbors and zoning municipality would love someone to come in and ask if that can now be townhouses or housing.

The neighbors usually don't want a warehouse. Many neighbors don't want industry or manufacturing in their area. Look for things you would have never looked for before. Look for opportunities in creation and development that would enrich the lives of the surrounding community. Often, the valuation of the property is created and enhanced the most at the beginning of the process with someone whose **eyes are wide open** to more possibilities.

One of my first developments had dilapidated trailers, two single lots, a big old house with the roof caving in, and an old greenhouse with broken glass. It was an 8-acre eyesore. I turned it into 24 lots and picked the builder. Those houses are now million-dollar homes right in the middle of town.

The Red Car Theory

If someone walked up to you and asked, "How many red cars did you see today?" you wouldn't be able to answer that question. You weren't looking for red cars.

If you were warned that you'd be asked that question, you would have red cars on your mind and be looking for them. You would have an answer when someone asked you.

This principle works for recognizing opportunities right in front of you that you couldn't see before. You likely drive by land every day that could be an opportunity, but you aren't paying attention. Just like the red cars, my goal is to have you seeing the opportunities around you by the end of this book!

Using the red car theory in land development sometimes means driving around looking for signs. This is something I like to do with my family, and we make a game out of it. When my daughter was very young, I would strap her into her car seat, pick up a coffee at the local shop, and we would drive around looking for signs. We spent many Saturdays taking road trips. It's a great way to get your family involved, and using apps like LandGlide, you can quickly check out properties and do the research you need when you get back.

It Gets Better...and Profitable

When you find the opportunities communities need in front of you, the possibilities are endless. But you have to know what to do, where to do it, and with whom.

- **In Chapter 7**, I take you through what you need to know to find builders and build long-lasting relationships with them. You need to be an asset, not someone who wastes their time.
- **In Chapter 8**, I show you how being a control freak pays off in the deals you make and relationships you establish. You need this if you want to gain control of that land.
- **In Chapter 9**, I help you know the ins and outs of building a strong marketing package. It's not that easy getting the deal with the builder if you don't have this down.
- **In Chapter 10**, I help you understand how to schedule meetings that get you the deals with the builders. You will want to read this chapter twice!
- **In Chapter 11**, we'll go through the money concerns you will face as a developer. You'll learn about options for getting the money you need and be introduced to creating value so you make more from your deals.
- **In Chapter 12**, we'll look at the different ways you can give your vote and use your voice to be an advocate for builders and buyers in your area.
- **In Chapter 13**, I simply show you how to not mess it up.

- **In Chapter 14**, we explore the community impact you make with your new revenue stream.

Are you ready to change your life, add a new stream of revenue to your business, and make a real impact in your community? Let's start by looking **at your market**.

CHAPTER 5

Know Your Market

No Shortcuts... Sorry

You are going to get a sneak peek into over 27 years of my experience in real estate. I've handled over a BILLION dollars worth of transactions in my career. I've seen the drawbacks of taking shortcuts and the surprising benefits of doing it right. Below are the two major mistakes developers make. Avoid these shortcuts and you're on the way to building a strong reputation as a developer.

> Remember, the goal is to stop being looked at as a cost and start being seen as a valued asset.

Shortcut Mistake #1:

Not understanding the zoning and not understanding what the planning department of that municipality will support.

If you fail to "underwrite" the land correctly, you set yourself up for a setback later. You may discover that the land isn't zoned correctly for what you have in mind. You may find you cannot get utilities and other essential needs to that land.

Shortcut Mistake #2:

You're not being a professional.

Imagine you're a real estate agent walking through a house you are showing. There are clear signs of water damage or dried-out water damage throughout the home. You look at the seller's report, and it says there's never been a roof leak. There's no problem, according to that report, so you sell the house to your buyer. Suddenly, the roof leaks and the buyer turns to you, saying, "You were my agent. You were supposed to protect me." They are stuck with $10,000 worth of damage, and they take you to court over it.

> Decide right now that you're going to be a professional.

Just like that real estate agent is held to standards of professionalism, so are you. Maybe you don't have to be licensed to be a developer, but if you are going to be one, do it right. Decide right now that you're going to be a professional. You're going to keep up with the news. You are going to watch for the articles on real estate, development, job announcements, etc.

You don't want someone coming back to you with: How did you not tell me there's about to be a new highway proposed in the backyard of this house?

Do The F*cking Work™ (DTFW™)

In this business, laziness can get you into big trouble and cost you a lot of money. You will need to have due diligence and an attitude that you're going to do the groundwork to ensure everything is going to happen as it should.

Your goal is to "see the future" and be able to capitalize on this, but you need to know your market. Here are some of the things you need to understand and the attitude you must take.

Get back to the basics.

This is not a social media-driven strategy—it's not for TikTok, Facebook, or Instagram. Being a successful developer is going off-screen—driving around in your vehicle and getting a feel for what is missing in the area.

You are going to be a thorough, hands-on developer who has done the work.

Your social media platform and website will not get you all the deals you need as a valued developer. In fact, depending on how you do your business, you may not even use these outreach methods at all. You are going to be a thorough, hands-on developer who has done the work.

Don't hide behind the email.

Back when I decided to branch out from the mortgage business, I did some speculation into development. I met up with a co-worker's relative, a general contractor. I simply proposed building a spec house together, and we did it. We took a little risk by getting the loan, but we found a lot, and he built the house. Then we built another and another. We ultimately made over $1,000,000 together.

This business takes face-to-face networking. It takes pounding the pavement and looking for opportunities. Furthermore, **Perfection is the enemy of progress.** Don't try to learn everything until it feels "safe" to start rolling the ball down the hill. Face your fear and get started early. Taking action will help you absorb what you learn more quickly.

The research builds your foundation.

I waited on tables in college and met my mentor at one of those tables. She owned a mortgage company, hired me, and taught me how to be a loan officer. When I walked in for my first day on the job, she handed me the Fannie Mae seller servicer guide, the FHA underwriting guide, the VA underwriting manual, and the USDA underwriting manual.

She made me read them all before I started my training to create a solid framework for success. I think of this learning system as creating a filing cabinet and files in your brain. When you see something, you know exactly where to go or where to put it.

Your future success with this process relies on you creating the filing cabinet and the files you need inside your brain. The most important thing you can do before starting anything else is to **read** the Unified Development Ordinance (UDO for your local city or county. It's the prerequisite training for learning this process.

Don't worry. We will help you create the folders as we go through this book. I got the idea of building cabinets and filing folders in your brain from my own early experience. It helped create a template inside my brain to properly receive the information at internal meetings or with a customer. I didn't have to memorize everything to understand the topics and follow along. When you create the files you'll store in your cabinets, you'll know what file to use as you utilize this system for your new revenue stream.

Don't skip this. DTFW™. The research and knowledge you gain will create the template for you to be ready to capitalize on things others don't think are possible. Even things you hadn't thought of before.

For example, I got a call from a builder one day asking for my help. One of the employees of one of his subcontractors was a plumber, and he wanted to buy a home in his development. He had his employer's permission to plumb the house at no cost to the builder. He wanted to know if he could do that.

It seemed far-fetched to me. I had never gotten this question before, but I had all those folders stored in my brain, and I recalled reading some provision covering sweat equity as a down payment. I knew right where to go, and sure enough, in an FHA transaction, a tradesperson can trade what would have been a builder cost for down payment. And that can act as part, or all, of the down payment requirement for FHA.

Most likely, that same phone call elsewhere would have resulted in them being told that's not something they can do. I had the framework in place that showed how this man could buy that house with no money down. It's the same with development.

You will read the Unified Development Ordinance and do the research beforehand. You'll be back in that red car theory, discovering opportunities you never knew existed. You will be ready to capitalize on things others don't consider possible.

Keeping up with your market is your profit.

Builders are so busy working in their businesses that they're not reading those articles. They're not always able to keep up with the news. Builders are relying on the developer to bring them those things.

It's your job to know the new traffic patterns and proposed zoning changes. You're the one who needs to be in the meetings with the planning boards or planning departments. Stay on top of what's happening now and what will happen in the future with the municipalities where you want to operate.

Solve bigger problems for better compensation.

If you want a stress-free job without problems, be a trash collector. You will solve someone else's problem by taking their trash, and you will be compensated accordingly.

When you solve the bigger problems, you will be compensated accordingly.

Solve the problems that deliver the most value to the prospective buyer of the lots you sell. Only then will you achieve your wealth goals. You're going to fill your folders with data through:

- Understanding watersheds.
- Studying zoning and projections.
- Conducting soils research.
- Understanding water availability.
- Understanding sewer availability.
- Exploring Department of Transportation (DOT) updates and planning.
- Keeping up on proposed plant closings and openings.
- Watching for new job announcements.

Meet with the economic development director for your area. What kind of businesses are they bringing in? Is there a lack of a certain type of housing stopping them from bringing in the businesses?

Now, you can take that to a builder that fits this need, letting them know you met with the economic development director, and they have this dire need. Give them the statistics and research on what they could sell that product for—what price and to which buyers. DTFW™!

It's not hard work, but it's work. NO cutting any corners to get there. It takes becoming a part of the market your land is going to serve.

Study the Unified Development Ordinance (UDO) for the county, town, or municipality. This is requirement #1 for getting into this process. It will be the foundation for everything that comes after.

Seek out the nonprofit associations for growth in your area. Join trade groups for builders and stay informed—research potential networking groups in your area. For example, in my area, we have a group called BASE, which stands for Business Alliance for Sound Economy. Business owners, real estate developers, brokers, and government officials come together in BASE.

Be a voracious reader of your local business journal and other publications. You want to read every association newsletter relevant to your market and every publication. This leads to the people you want to connect with within these materials, as well as inspiration on what's missing from your area.

Study the town's vision of where the growth is going and how it will change over time. This may be a Vision 2030 statement and video representation. When you see land that's not zoned the way it should be, you will have the tools you need at the public hearing. Often, all you need is this vision statement and the UDO.

Possible scenario:

Armed with the knowledge of the UDO and the vision statement, you find a large tract that meets all the needs. You take this to a builder and propose that you work together.

"I see you're building a couple hundred houses here a year. Look at this 100-acre tract. It's right in the path of the town's 2030 vision statement. They want townhouses, medium density, of this and this. By the way, you're building all of this. What if we get control of this together? What if I go and get it planned based on your footprint sizes for your townhouses? I think they're going to sell. Here's the data, and I've got a sign-off from planning that they would support this."

You flip the contract to the builder and get some cash flow coming into your business. If you want to be more involved, that's common too. You can control it up to putting the water, sewer, and infrastructure in place. You can hire the utility and other contractors from start to finish. You're a developer with options.

Read the UDO and learn about the municipality's vision and forecasted plan for the market. Study the traffic today and the projected changes. Understand where the schools are, where new districts will happen in the future, and all the shifts in the areas throughout the town.

By the time you get through everything, you are a welcomed asset and you put together a proposal for a builder to buy from you. You're bringing the vision of what this land can become to life and making the builder's job 100% easier. CREATE VALUE!

It's Time to Own It

Own the title of developer and attach it to your name everywhere. Print out business cards with your new title. Create a brand that says, "We Buy Land!"

Don't let people love you into a lower level.

Usually, those people who are closer to you worry too much. For example, you know what Mom is like. She wants you to be careful and surround you in bubble wrap so the world never hurts you. Some of that is good, but you will never live to your full potential. The people around you will likely try to love you to a lower level. It's okay to fire people who think they're architects of your life. You don't even have to tell them! I think I fired my entire family sometime between ten and twelve years old. I love them all but knew I wanted something different than what they had in life.

You have your framework in place. You hung out your developer "sign." **Now it's time to get some land and build your new revenue stream.** Let's look at what constitutes a Good Piece Of Land™" and how you should handle that phase of your business.

Go to www.impactful-development.com/bonuses to register and download free bonusses

CHAPTER 6

Understanding and Finding A Good Piece Of Land™

Note: Make sure you are working on this at the same time as you do the steps in the previous chapters.

What Is a Good Piece Of Land™?

A Good Piece Of Land™ is one that fits all the requirements needed to do what you want with it for the end user. Here is a checklist of what defines a Good Piece Of Land™ and what does not.

You want land that has the following:

- The ability to have water, sewer, and power.
  - From a municipal perspective, you must be able to put a septic tank on it, drill a well on it, or have water and sewer availability.

- A stable surface area that can be built upon.
  - You don't want something on the side of a mountain or too close to water where sand shifts. Will the soils handle the weight bearing of a house?
- Proper zoning in place or the ability to rezone.
  - Make sure the land has the proper zoning for what you intend to do with it or that it can be rezoned.

Avoid land that has the following:

- Anything contrary to the above.
- Lack of proximity to infrastructure.
- Protected area for an endangered species.
- A cemetery is on the tract.
- A building location set within a flood zone.

How to Find Your Land

Here is where DTFW™ comes into play again. You are going to go out and find your land. Land doesn't just come to you. Most of the time, you're employing the red car theory and seeking out those opportunities that you've been blind to before.

Drive around and keep your eyes open for anything that turns a piece of land into a Good Piece Of Land™. Look for manholes on the roads. Where are the nearest fire hydrants? What utilities are on the poles? Sometimes, you may be looking for natural gas posts that say "Natural gas line. Don't cut here."

You're looking for a lack of infrastructure. You don't want that—it can kill your plans and come back to bite you hard.

A bad piece of land will be in flood zones, and the soil will be too weak to withstand building. You're looking for those types of gaps. (Extensive checklists are available in the course.)

One possible scenario could be seeing a section of land with greenery, trees, and nothing else. On either side of it is a neighborhood and maybe a shopping center. There's a subdivision and traffic lights. What's going on with that land? Who owns it?

You have read the articles, the nonprofit newsletters, the market news, the manuals, and the vision plan. You believe you have a good understanding of the market. Now, your radar is fully tuned in as you drive around, and you're looking for the gaps that will provide you with the best opportunities.

Where are the gaps? What's out of place? What's missing? You drive through an area of 8,000 people and notice it doesn't have a car wash. You see a tract of empty land in the perfect location for that car wash. You check out the water and sewer and zoning. You get control of the tract of land and resell it to the nearby car wash guys by giving them all the details that prove they can make money there. You both make money.

Look around for gaps and fill them!

Where are the choke points in freeway traffic? Engage yourself and get excited when you're stuck on the freeway. Look around for those gaps and needs. Where are all these people driving to and from? What are they driving past that could potentially have homes or apartments telling them, "You could live here now. You could be home by now."

Where are the choke points off the freeway? Learn the market and discover opportunities to fill the pressing needs. What are their most pressing needs when they're at this point? Or can I get them home before this point?

Another potential opportunity is dilapidated buildings. Is there an old house falling down in the middle of a wooded area? DTFW™ and get all the information you need. Go a step further and familiarize yourself with the county's Geographic Information System (GIS).

Use the tools at hand.

Get in the market to find the opportunities, and then use the tools available to move the process forward. You may use some of these tools and others.

- Google Maps/Earth helps you see what is happening and lets you plan your land discovery car ride that day. (Personally, I find just jumping in the car and spending the day in the market more beneficial than planning my route.)
- LandGlide is a program for your phone that tells you a lot of what you need to know about a property. (Currently $99/year)
- GIS - you'll have to do some digging to understand how to search property by address, by the owner, by tax

parcel ID number, and how to navigate the county's real estate, tax records, and GIS system.

Discovery Through Leveraging Relationships

I have a special Bonus for you. We will experience the most massive shift of asset transformation that's ever occurred from one generation to another. Statistics show that 10,000 baby boomers are retiring per day.[13] These assets, including land, will be transferred to the next generation, and they will usually want the cash!

You can find these opportunities through building relationships with estate planning attorneys. I suggest you also build relationships with divorce attorneys and bankruptcy attorneys. Building connections with attorneys is a great way to cover the Three D's of real estate: Death, Divorce, and Destitution.

> You may discover that you're a solution to their current problem!

Leverage these relationships to help you discover land opportunities that may not be as visible. These people understand what's involved with the current ownership of this land. When you see a deserted and forgotten tract, you may discover that you're a solution to their current problem!

---

[13] Scates, J. (2023, May 31). The impact of Baby Boomers retiring in 2023. The Impact of Baby Boomers Retiring in 2023. https://www.j2t-recruiting.com/post/the-impact-of-baby-boomers-retiring-in-2023

Create connections with:

- **Estate attorneys:** You can help a family close out the estate and provide liquidity.
- **Divorce attorneys:** You can help them out with any excess land. (Bonus cash flow tip: this relationship works for acquiring rental property.)
- **Bankruptcy attorneys:** People need to sell land quickly, and this lawyer is often involved in resolving these stressful situations and helping them move on with life.
- **Small Business CPAs:** 6-8% of baby boomers own businesses that many of their heirs don't want. These assets often include extra land. Business owners may have excess land because they're not growing their business anymore.
- **Insurance agents:** They often know what issues their clients have that can be relieved by letting go of some land, or they can point you to someone who's getting ready to sell.
- **Financial planners:** These people can have the same insights as others on this list.
- **Other real estate developers**: Partnering with another developer with a good reputation working with the same builders can prove lucrative.
- **Local and state politicians.**

Leverage relationships with brokers.

One rule: don't take a referral fee.

Even if you're a broker, don't take referral fees if you're the buyer. If you're a broker and you ask other brokers to bring you things, they'll bring them to you last because they make less money. I have brokers in my connections, and they know if they call me, I will let them represent me for full commission. I don't take a penny of it. I want them to bring me the best properties they find.

> Example networking script for broker to broker:
>
> "I'm expanding my business, and I'm going to start doing some developments in this area. I'm looking for lots and tracts of land that meet these needs. I don't want a referral fee. If you're representing the seller, I'll represent myself. If the seller is represented, you can represent me and earn the full commission."

This works for me. I have brokers who bring me good pieces of property and bring them to me early. They know I can perform, and they get their full commission. It's a win-win!

Remember, once you find the land through these relationships, you still need to identify whether or not it is a Good Piece Of Land™. Once you verify that the land meets your needs using the checklist in the course, it's time to find a builder.

Go to www.impactful-development.com/bonuses to register and download free bonusses

CHAPTER 7

What if You're a Homebuilder?

Are you a small homebuilder who buys finished lots? Good news! You can expand your business like any other real estate professional by developing your own lots.

Improve Your Margin as You Develop Your Own Inventory™

Typically, a developer makes anywhere between 25 and 50% markup on the creation of a lot and then sells it to a homebuilder. You can create a new revenue stream within your home construction business by developing your own lots and making that margin for yourself instead.

Stop waiting for something great to come on the market. Get out there and make it happen now. Level out your business model by creating your own lot inventory to build homes on.

Chapter 6 explains how to find a Good Piece Of Land™ aimed at real estate professionals. As a builder, you're more familiar with how a lot will or will not work. You will be a step ahead of real estate agents, but that doesn't mean you can be lazy here. You still need to DTFW™ when it comes to going out and finding your land.

The land isn't going to just come to you. You will have to employ that red car theory and seek out those opportunities. When you locate a Good Piece Of Land™ with a promising infrastructure, you find an opportunity you were blind to before.

Investigate Based on Your Builder's Expertise

If you're a high-end homebuilder, you're obviously looking at different pieces of property than if you're an entry-level homebuilder. Your needs may be more defined than those of some real estate professionals, but you can utilize the same principles within the book to impact your building business in the same way.

You'll use your builder's expertise to investigate potential areas ideal for building homes. You'll locate signs of water, such as manholes on the road. You'll see what utilities are available in the area by looking at poles and checking for signs of access to natural gas. You'll be on the lookout for fire hydrant access, and make note of where that is in relation to the land.

The checklists available in my latest course will help you be as thorough as possible with this process. They will help you remember to identify infrastructure gaps that make it a bad piece of land, such as the land being in a flood zone. You don't want to miss gaps like those that can kill your plans and come back to bite you hard.

DTFW™ and Don't Rush Things

First, make sure you adopt the right mindset. In Chapter 3, we look at the difference between a missionary entrepreneur and a mercenary one. You must be a missionary entrepreneur for this process to work. Don't skip Chapter 3.

Second, understand that when you investigate the land, you also need to understand the market. In this business, laziness can get you into big trouble and cost you a lot of money. You will need to conduct your due diligence and have an attitude that you're going to do the groundwork to ensure everything is going to happen as it should.

Your goal is to "see the future" and be able to capitalize on this, but you need to know your market. Here are some of the things you need to understand and the attitude you must take.

The same rules that apply to everyone else, also apply to you: NO Shortcuts.

> The same rules that apply to everyone else, also apply to you: NO Shortcuts.

Avoid These Two Mistakes

Mistake #1:

Not understanding the zoning and not understanding what the planning department of that municipality will support.

If you fail to "underwrite" the land correctly, you set yourself up for a setback later. You may discover that the land isn't zoned correctly for what you have in mind. You may find you cannot get utilities and other essential needs to that land.

Mistake #2:

You're not being a professional.

Imagine you're a real estate agent walking through a house you are showing. There are clear signs of water damage or dried-out water damage throughout the home. You look at the seller's report, and it says there's never been a roof leak. There's no problem, according to that report, so you sell the house to your buyer. Suddenly, the roof leaks and the buyer turns to you, saying, "You were my buyer's agent. You were supposed to protect me." They are stuck with $10,000 worth of damage, and they take you to court over it.

> Decide right now that you're going to be a professional.

Just like that real estate agent is held up to standards of professionalism, so are you. If you are going to be a developer, do it right. Decide right now that you're going to be a professional. You're going to keep up with the news. You are going to watch for the articles on real estate, development, job announcements, etc.

You don't want someone coming back to you with: How did you not tell me there's about to be a new highway proposed in the backyard of this house?

Research Builds Your Foundation

I waited on tables in college and met my mentor at one of those tables. She owned a mortgage company, hired me, and taught me how to be a loan officer. When I walked in for my first day on the job, she handed me the Fannie Mae seller servicer guide, the FHA underwriting guide, the VA underwriting manual, and the USDA underwriting manual.

She made me read them all before I started my training to create a solid framework for success. I think of this learning system as creating a filing cabinet and files in your brain. When you see something, you know exactly where to go or where to put it.

Your future success with this process relies on you creating the filing cabinet and the files you need inside your brain. The most important thing you can do before starting anything else is to read the Unified Development Ordinance (UDO) for your local city or county. It's the prerequisite training for learning this process.

Don't worry. We will help you create the folders as we go through this book. I got the idea of building cabinets and filing folders in your brain from my own early experience. It helped create a template inside my brain to properly receive the information at internal meetings or with a customer. I didn't have to memorize everything to understand the topics and follow along. When you create the files you'll store in your cabinets, you'll know what file to use as you utilize this system for your new revenue stream.

Don't skip this. DTFW™.

The research and knowledge you gain will create the template for you to be ready to capitalize on things others don't think are possible. Even things you hadn't thought of before.

For example, I got a call from a builder one day asking for my help. One of the employees of one of his subcontractors was a plumber, and he wanted to buy a home in his development. He had his employer's permission to plumb the house at no cost to the builder. He wanted to know if he could do that.

It seemed far-fetched to me. I had never gotten this question before, but I had all those folders stored in my brain, and I recalled reading some provision covering sweat equity as a down payment. I knew right where to go, and sure enough, in an FHA transaction, a tradesperson can trade what would have been a builder cost for a down payment. And that can act as part, or all, of the down payment requirement for FHA.

Most likely, that same phone call elsewhere would have resulted in them being told that's not something they can do. I had the framework in place that showed how this man could buy that house with no money down. It's the same with development.

If you will read the UDO and do the research beforehand, you'll be back in that red car theory, discovering opportunities you never knew existed. You will be ready to capitalize on things others don't consider possible.

Keeping up with your market is your profit.

Remember, you're the developer now. It's your job to know the new traffic patterns and proposed zoning changes. You're the one who needs to be in the meetings with the planning boards or planning departments. Stay on top of what's happening now and what will happen in the future with the municipalities where you want to operate.

> Your goal is to "see the future" and be able to capitalize on this.

By adopting some of the principles in Impactful Development found throughout this book, you can impact your homebuilding company in a substantially positive way.

- Create another revenue stream for your business by building your own lot inventory.
- Positively impact communities by providing a solution to the housing problems facing them.
- Positively impact your future and your family's future.

Although many of the chapters are not specifically written for a homebuilder who is also a developer, the information inside each one is valuable to you. As the developer, you will take on duties and activities usually done by a real estate professional.

The course that is the companion to this book dives into the different ways you can impact your home construction business in more detail. You can check it out now at impactful-development.com and get all the checklists and training that come with it. The coaching available to you with that course will be customized to fit your business situation and goals to prevent you from making mistakes that jeopardize your future revenue.

CHAPTER 8

Finding Builders

Note: You should be working on this at the same time as everything we discussed in the previous chapters.

DTFW™...Again!

You have to work at this, but it's not hard work. Be thorough—this is another place you do not want to take shortcuts. Failure to do proper research before contacting a builder will endanger your reputation as a developer.

Know the builders well BEFORE you get to know them in person. Be absolutely sure that the builder is actively building the types of properties you're finding land for before you contact them. You want everyone to take your phone call. You want every builder in your market to know your name when they see it. You want them to instantly feel you will not waste their time with something they won't be interested in looking at.

> You want them to instantly feel you will not waste their time with something they won't be interested in looking at.

Start by Googling the top ten builders in your market area. Chart those builders, find out what subdivisions they are in, and drive to those. Look at what they do. Does the builder specialize in vinyl boxes, massive houses, affordable housing, or what? Choose the ones building what you wish to specialize in, and find land to form a strong relationship.

Get to know the smaller builders and modular/mobile home dealers in your market. You don't have to go after the big guys. Go back to the habit of DTFW™ and start researching all your potential builder connections. There's no need to overthink this and overcomplicate the process. Don't overthink any of it and talk yourself out of adding a lucrative pipeline to your business. Keep It Simple. (Follow the K.I.S.S. method throughout this book.)

Simple tracking is all you need.

I like to create an Excel spreadsheet to keep track of the builders in my market. Simply enter the information to help you validate a land's potential for that builder's needs. Use this information to determine what size of lots you will need, what type of buildings you can research for them, and get an idea of how much they would pay you for those lots. (A spreadsheet is included in the course.)

At a glance, you'll see the answers to the following questions:

- How many houses did they sell last year?
- What was their average sales price?
- What was the average square footage of their builds?
- What are the average lot sizes they build on?
- What type of locations/neighborhoods do they build in?
- What/where are they actively building now?
- How much are they paying for their current lots?

Connecting With Builders

Now, it's time to pick up the phone and shake hands. Get out, connect with the builders in your market, and form those relationships. Join the local builders association and network with them at the next event.

Simple conversations often turn into money-making deals.

Builder: What do you do?
You: I develop real estate.
Builder: Oh, where?
You: All over the area. What area are you interested in?

Be direct and helpful without worrying about how good or smart you look. They love connecting at these events and appreciate developers who don't overcomplicate processes or conversations.

Meeting a builder for the first time is a lot like dating. Just like with speed dating, you'll meet a few you want to meet for a second date. One builder may be rude and a complete jerk when you meet him. Another builder might be warm and friendly, leaving you after that first conversation thinking, "I want to find out more about that builder and take this to the next step."

> It's okay not to do business with someone who gives you a bad feeling.

It's okay not to do business with someone who gives you a bad feeling. In fact, I suggest you do not do business with them. Sure, give someone who may be having a rough day a second chance, but if you consistently get a bad feeling about someone, move along to the next builder.

Chapter Recap:

The tricks to building successful connections with builders in your area are...

- Know the builder before you get to know them in person.
- Make the phone calls and meet them where they hang out. Print out the d*mn business cards.
- Keep It Simple. They are as busy as you are. Get right to the point and find out what they need most for their lots.
- Taking action is better than doing nothing. Just "own it" and DTFW™.
- Relax. You're not getting married to them. Think of it as speed dating.

- Understand that you may not get along with everyone. That's okay.
- Be real and do business with people you like for a more profitable future together.

Don't worry about what happens next. Remember, you're a professional developer in the real estate business. Own it. You're going to control the land. Let me show you how in Chapter 9.

CHAPTER 9

Be a Control Freak™ - It's Time to Control The Land

The Broker vs. Developer Mentality

A land broker and a land developer have two very different viewpoints on selling land and how they earn a profit. Let me break it down for you, so you can adopt the developer mentality and get more out of your business.

A broker is straight up about selling the land to the builder. A broker will see a tract of land on the market for half a million. For a 3% commission on $500,000, a broker will present this to a builder. A builder who DTFW™ knows the zoning, the water, and the sewer, and understands this land is worth $750,000. The broker mentality is being excited about making that $15,000 in their brokerage fee as presented.

On the other hand, a developer who DTFW™ knows the land is worth $750,000 and says, "Let me control this land!" That developer gets a water service letter and a sewer service letter to show there's water, sewer, and power. The developer talks to the planning development about zoning and how many lots can fit on that land. With a little research on the builder, the developer will see how much they've been paying per acre or lot. That developer puts together a marketing package for the builder, to which the builder sees the land is worth $750,000 and offers the developer $700,000.

A broker just wants to sell a piece of land and make a percentage off that sale, while a developer creates or uncovers value in the land and makes a lot more money by becoming a control freak. **In the above illustration, the broker took in $15,000 while the developer took in $200,000.**

> **Note:** An ethical, professional developer does not overprice or extract more than the value they have figured out how to create or more than the value they have discovered in a property. They maximize and are good stewards of their assets but don't get greedy.

Remember, the builder welcomes the developer relationship. They expect you to make a profit. You have done a ton of work and saved them from having to do it, giving them more time to concentrate on building homes. A developer—you—is on a mission to solve a problem and get paid for it.

Control Equals Value Creation

You don't have to own the land to promote it, but you do need to control it before you promote it. The offer you make will be based on the potential you see in the land. There are different ways to control the land that I'll lightly describe for you here.

> **Money Matters Note:** You may have the cash on hand and that's great. Depending on how you gain control, you may need to put up a refundable or non-refundable deposit. If you don't have the cash on hand, we will talk about ways to find investors and borrow money in a later chapter.

Control Method #1: Traditional Contract

In a traditional contract situation, you get the property under your control by settling on a price and making a deposit. During the examination period, you continue your investigation of the property's full potential. Of course, you have already done some before this point, but now you're finishing up your DTFW™ so you can offer this land to a builder.

Equitable Title Rights

Check your state laws for "equitable title" rules. In this case, you do not own the land, but because you are under contract for a piece of property you can promote it. You have to disclose that you don't have ownership of the land yet when you present your offer to people. Make sure your contract is assignable.

With a traditional contract, you may have to put money down or you may not. There's a myth that people believe that it can't be a contract if it doesn't involve a deposit. It actually can. Typically, you would put a refundable deposit held in escrow, though.

Control Method #2: Option Contract

You give the land owner a non-refundable deposit for the option to buy the land from them at a specified price and within a specified time period. There's no obligation to close on it, but the right to close on it is secured. Most options are recorded in the courthouse, and the seller cannot legally sell it to anyone else because you have an option on it. This locks the property up and you can offer it to prospective buyers for an assignment fee.

Control Method #3: Seller-Held Financing

If the seller doesn't owe anything on the land, you may choose to offer a small down payment and the seller agrees to handle financing it to you on contract. Maybe the seller inherited a tract of land you feel has potential. You offer that person $5000 down and a specified payment amount each month over an agreed upon number of months.

> **Note:** Do your due diligence and understand seller financing rights in your state.

Laws on seller-held financing vary from state to state. Do your due diligence and understand seller financing rights in your state. Many states have laws to help prevent unscrupulous sellers from marking properties up by a substantial amount.

For instance, in North Carolina, seller financing is non-recourse. They can't come after you for a deficiency balance if they were the seller of the property. So if you overinflated a property, took someone's down payment, and then they can't afford it anymore, you can't sue them for a deficiency balance. All you can do is get the deed back.

Control Method #4: Traditional Purchase

You have some cash on hand and see land you want, so you buy the land for cash. You own and control the land. You possess the deed.

> **Note:** The content in this book does not constitute legal advice, nor does it substitute for legal advice. Check the guidelines in your state for laws covering land control, financing, buying, and selling, and consult with an attorney.

Introducing Your Advanced Training

Our goal here is to present you with the options and the ways to Be a Control Freak™. This chapter gives you the basic knowledge of how to gain control of land. Because this topic is so complex and full of details, I cannot cover it all in this book.

However, I have put together a system to help you get additional advice and more information on being a lucrative land developer. Join me at impactful-development.com to see your options or apply for my 1-to-1 coaching opportunities.

CHAPTER 10

Putting Together Your Good Piece Of Land™ Marketing Package

Pulling Your DTFW™ Together

This is where you validate all your DTFW™ materials for the builder to whom you wish to make an offer. You should have researched the builder by now, and you understand their products. Dive deeper to get a good sense of what they need and how to customize your marketing piece.

> They don't want a lot of options and will not allow a lot of changes.

You looked at their neighborhoods. You understand the product they build and what size of footprints they need. You made sure the land you want to sell them fits with what they're building. Most non-custom builders like to build the same thing over and over again. They know their costs, who their subs are, and exactly what to do. They don't want a lot of options and will not allow a lot of changes.

You want to be able to come to that builder and say something like, "You built this neighborhood with this type of product, and the biggest footprint in that product line was 40 feet wide by 70 feet deep to handle the whole house. I have a neighborhood of 50 lots. I've already verified that your typical footprint of this product line already fits these lots."

If you're a REALTOR®, you will provide what's typically called the competitive market analysis (CMA) for those homes. You would add, "By the way, here's a marketing analysis of what these houses look like and what they would sell for at this location."

Perhaps your research shows that the average selling price for these houses in their neighborhoods is $400,000. You're offering the lots at $72,000, 18% of their final sales price. After presenting that, you show the research you've done on the builder's typical requirements and add, "We know the metric you want to stay between is 20 and 25% at the most, so these lots really add value to your future sales."

What if you're not a REALTOR®?

You can still provide the CMA but in a different way. Instead of presenting the CMA, you change your statement to say, "I took a look at your typical product line and had this in mind."

Building Your Marketing Package

Have your marketing package completed for the builder to review and help seal the deal for your land. Include the CMA if you're a REALTOR®; if not, leave that out and give that statement of your vision above during your introduction, or partner with a great REALTOR® in your market. Fill out your marketing package with the following items:

- Average selling price of the product line.
- Lot price, showing the anticipated percentage cost of the total sales price.
- The documentation showing that you've done due diligence on water and sewer capacity.
- Distances showing the proximity of resources relevant to the demographic for that neighborhood.
- Wetlands, soils analysis, surveys, and other materials from your DTFW™ for the land.
- Zoning classification of the land showing that it currently meets the preliminary site plan or a letter from the planning department that would show support for the site plan approval.

Include the preliminary site plan you propose, and say to the builder, "Here is my proposed preliminary site plan if you're seriously interested in this tract. I would love your input on this site plan based on your product line or your choice before I move forward to get approval."

When you include the builder on the site plan, you allow them to feel "ownership" of the land with you. You get them involved early on in the process and create an implied commitment on their part in many cases. If the builder is already giving input on the planning and you're making changes at their request before they're even committed to buying it, you're planting the seed of future ownership.

> They will feel a sense of ownership early on and will want to make sure they're the one who buys it from you.

For this reason, you want to refer to it as a preliminary site plan. You give your target buyers a hook that they bite on by letting them have input. They will feel a sense of ownership early on and will want to make sure they're the one who buys it from you.

Pull The Trigger

Now it is your turn. It's time to get out there and create that pipeline that provides solutions for you, the builder, and the community. There are no excuses here. You did the work, and you have created value. There is nothing to fear other than what you will miss out on if you do nothing.

> **No risk, no reward. Not true!**
>
> Just like you do not have to start big, you also do not have to start with substantial risk. Don't listen to those who say no risk = no reward. You can still make great returns while mitigating risk. In development, you DTFW™ to reduce your risk to almost zero when you can and by a substantial amount at other times.

We go through several key strategies in the course to help mitigate your risks and protect the downsides. Trusting in the process will help you earn bigger rewards when you DTFW™.

That's it. If you have all of the above, you are ready to talk to builders. In the next chapter, we'll show you how to move the builder to the next step and get your deal closed. Don't skip this next chapter. It's so important you'll want to **read it twice**!

CHAPTER 11

Selling Your "Good Piece Of Land™" to a Builder

Read This Chapter Twice!

Setting the Meeting

You get the meetings with builders because you can articulate the fit of your land to that builder. You are able to say, "I have this piece of land, and I noticed from your other neighborhoods that you've had great success building on lots like these."

Be the control freak™. You control the land. **Call it yours.**

You want to be face-to-face. These types of deals are best accomplished when they're in person. Zoom, email, and Facebook don't work as well. Someone committing millions of dollars to a transaction wants to look you in the eyes and feel that you know what you are doing.

Relax. It's all good.

Compare meeting face-to-face to weightlifting. Lifting weights is uncomfortable, but you get better after a while, and you look pretty damn good after a consistent effort. So, if you struggle in your first meetings, if no one buys, but you've learned something, that's a win. Adopt a mentality of win or learn—there's no failure.

Next time, you will do it better. The time after that, you will improve more, and again after that. You'll leave a meeting at some point, thinking, "I nailed it! They're going to buy." That may be the first meeting, or it may be the 10th, but trust the process. You'll get there.

It doesn't happen overnight.

Development may take you on an emotional rollercoaster ride. You get the guts to make the first offer and it does not work out. It hits you where you feel most uncertain and you think perhaps you're not cut out for this. You don't go to the gym for one day and give up, saying it didn't work for you. You have to keep taking action and remember it's a numbers game. There's no real ratio of the pieces of land you look at to the ones you end up controlling. You may find one good one in a few that you check out, or you may look at properties for two months before you find one.

Use wise time management.

Shoot for 10-30 minutes for the meeting. Respect their time and let them know in detail what to expect beforehand. Then, make sure you can fit it all in, including questions they may ask, for the time frame you gave them.

Example script to get you started:

I need 18 minutes of your time to show you a project I know a lot about that I think you'll be super interested in. It's very similar to this project you've already built and successfully sold out. If you give me 18 minutes of your time, I will show you something that can replicate the success you've already had.

Let them be the driver. Keep the meeting scheduled within your proposed time frame and allow them to be the ones to ask for more time if they want more.

Conducting the Meeting

Steven Covey used a great demonstration with *The Seven Habits of Highly Effective People*. He put an empty jar on a table, and he put a pitcher of water, a pitcher of sand, some small pebbles, some medium rocks, and some large rocks on the table. He then asked people to fit them inside the jar.

They tried. Each one found it impossible to fit everything into the jar. "Let me show you how it's done," Steven said when they gave up.

He put the large rocks in first, then the medium rocks, and he shook the jar to settle them. Then he took the small pebbles and settled those in. Then he took the sand and shook the jar to settle that in. And then, he slowly poured the water in, and it all fit.

The moral of the story? Always put the big rocks in first.

The same goes for your meeting. Talk about the site plan first. Show how the zoning is correct. Talk about how the water capacity lines up right. Show the water pressure is what the fire marshal will require. Point out the water treatment and sewer/septic tank and the soils report.

Start with the big things first. The smaller, more detailed will naturally flow toward the end when they're more interested. That's when they should start asking questions.

Questions are a good thing.

Novice developers often mistake questions as a sign of skepticism when they actually indicate a sign of interest. If they are genuinely interested in the property, they will ask a lot of questions. The more questions they ask, the more value you can provide.

Get comfortable saying, "I don't know, but I'll find out." In fact, make an effort to draw out more questions from them. The more answers you can find for them, the more valuable your offer becomes to them during the follow-up. Take amazing notes as the meeting goes along because when you're taking notes, that's a sign of professionalism.

At this stage, you should know the big rocks and some of the medium rocks. You don't have to know all the medium rocks, all the pebbles, all the sand, or all the water. You can make a solid professional impression by making the extra effort to find details for the follow-up.

Perfection is the Enemy of Progress™. Move things forward! Let the builder know you will be back with the answers to their questions. Give yourself plenty of time to get all the information they need. Don't rush it, and don't make the follow-up time a definite date, or you risk setting yourself up for failure.

Example of what to say about following up with them:

I've taken note of all your questions and will follow up with you. Many of these answers require third-party feedback. I will try to get back to you within a week or give you an update on what I'm waiting on.

Remember to get the builder's input on that site plan during the meeting. You should already have had their feedback from before and implemented that into the preliminary site plan. This is an excellent time to ask them if they thought of anything else to strengthen their sense of ownership in the land.

Post-Meeting Review

Take the time to evaluate the conversation after the meeting so you can improve each time.

If they weren't interested, what's your after-battle action plan? What can you learn by answering these questions?

- Why didn't they buy?
- What questions did they ask that I didn't know the answers to?
- What are the things I could have done better?
- What things didn't I prepare well enough?
- What are the questions I could have anticipated?

If they are interested, review everything and locate ways to do better at the next meeting with a builder.

- What did I learn from the meeting?
- What was I missing?
- What could I have done better?
- What did they ask that I didn't have an answer to?
- Do I need to revise my marketing package based on this conversation?

This after-meeting debrief reminds me of when you list residential real estate and put it under contract. The house is under contract for the first time, and you have a disclosure. In our state, it's a residential property disclosure. Do you know if anything is wrong with the property? Don't disclose that, and you can be sued.

Things like this can happen. The first person goes under contract, and they hire an independent home inspector. They get a home inspection, and the prospective buyer submits it with a repair request. The seller says, "No way I'm doing all that stuff." Is there a revision to the disclosure now? Because you now know everything that's wrong with the property, there should be.

Similarly, there should be a revision to your marketing package now because you know what will come up next time that you didn't cover this time.

Follow Up With the Builder and Close

Work efficiently to gather your responses to all concerns and questions based on the initial meeting with the builder. Ask the builder if the responses are good or if they need additional information before moving forward to a contract. If yes, respond as fast as possible to answer the questions and move it forward.

Feel the sense of urgency.

All opportunities are like melting ice cream cones. While you are a control freak™ in acquiring the land and while meeting with the builder to get it under contract, think of those ice cream cones. People tend to wait and move too slowly when that opportunity exists. That opportunity suddenly becomes that ice cream cone you didn't consume quick enough that's melted in your hands and you have nothing left. There should be a sense of urgency to everything you do.

Get a proposed agreement in front of the builder as fast as possible. When giving a price, use the term "this is a guidance price." There's a nuance in the difference between providing an offering price and a guidance price. A guidance price protects you if there's a multiple-offer situation.

Most people will ask you, "What is a guidance price?" You can respond with, "It's a guidance price because I have no idea how long you're going to ask me to take to close. If you close in 30 days, that price may differ from when you ask for six months to close. If you ask me to get every approval, engineering, and permits, that price will be different than if you prefer to handle it on your own."

Something as simple as using a "guidance price" can help solidify trust between you and the builder. It enables you to anticipate future asks that you cannot control.

If they question any price changes, you can show them how it's a price based upon all the other terms of the offer. That's important in the unemotional land and builder transactions, and it will help them feel safe coming back to you on your next deal, even if they didn't get the first one, without animosity.

Negotiation Examination Period

During this phase, you will be negotiating the "seller deliverables."

Will the buyer take the land as it is now? In this case, the builder takes the land as it is zoned, as it stands. They'll hire the engineer and get the stormwater, water extension, department of transportation, and other permits they need.

Or does the buyer expect you to spend $100,000+ and get all that done first? In these deals, you must be familiar with the time frames of acquiring the seller deliverables. It varies by location. It may be eight to ten months, or it could be a process that takes three years plus!

Don't worry. If you need more help understanding this, I go in-depth with these negotiations and how to set things up in the course.

The bottom line is that it's critically important that you understand seller deliverables before accepting an offer. Both as a buyer in what you want the seller to provide and as a seller so you understand what the buyer is asking you to provide.

Bulls make money, bears make money, and hogs get slaughtered.

- Wall Street Term

Don't be a hog. **You're playing this for the long term, making it extremely important to develop a reputation of fairness. Be a missionary entrepreneur, not a mercenary one.** You're more interested in providing more value to your buyer than the price they paid.

You're Not Done After You Sell

Continue to build the relationships after the closing.

The developer mentality continually works to deepen the existing relationships and keep that revenue pipeline full. I have recurring planning meetings with my larger clients, their key people and chief financial officers, or the people who control the money and owners. I show you how you can schedule these monthly or quarterly planning meetings with your largest, best clients that lead to more sales in my course!

In fact, while I'm writing this, I know my next task today is to prepare for a meeting tomorrow with a client I've closed over $150,000,000 in transactions. We're going to discuss each other's goals at this meeting. I'm more concerned with how I can be of service than what I can take. Builders love meeting with people who have a service mentality, returning to how you should be a missionary entrepreneur in everything you do.

Are you a real estate professional?

In many cases, the acquisition contract of the land or the lot should include a clause requiring the builder to list the end product with you and your firm, provided your state's real estate guidelines allow that via disclosure in the contract.

What if you're not a real estate professional?

You are going to monitor absorption after the closing. You are going to assess how many a month they are selling.

For instance, let's say you sold them 120 lot subdivisions, and they're selling five a month. That means they're going to sell out in two years. You need to get another similar neighborhood in front of them at least six to twelve months before that to replace that successful transaction.

By doing this, you're also providing a valuable service in solving a problem the builder doesn't know they have yet. Many builders fail at anticipating absorptions and keeping their pipeline full of projects that might be one, two, and three years out.

It's your job to DTFW™ for them, to bring enthusiasm, and to solve a problem before it hits. You will be able to say, "I've been monitoring sales in that neighborhood. I'm so happy for you. Are you pleased with how many you're selling per month?"

If they say no, ask, "What could we have done differently to improve your sales, so I know for next time?"

If they say yes, that's your cue to move them to the next step. "Great! I'm already working on several replacement neighborhoods based on the timing of when you should be sold out. I would like to set up a follow-up meeting with you. I'll be back in touch to let you know when I am ready to show you a presentation similar to the last one. We can replace that neighborhood and make sure you keep those sales going!"

Words matter. Notice that in the above script, I use the word "we." You want to be an asset to them, viewed as a "partner!"

Bonus Outreach Goal

If being a developer is your long-term goal, make following up with your clients an annual event. I do a Crush The New Year party every year on the third week of January with my clients and my team.

This works for two reasons. First, I'm filling pipelines for my builder clients at two, three, and four years out. And second, if you're in this for the long term, your builder should expect a call to ask questions like, "What is your goal for this year? Where are your gaps? How can I seek to help fill them for you?"

You should know every one of your builder clients, their annual goals for closings, and how many houses they want to build that year. It doesn't matter if they want to build 12 or 1200 houses. Most of you will have both large and small builders in your market.

It's absolutely critical that you align yourself to understand their individual goals and help them fill that need. They look at you as a partner versus a salesperson. Even if they're a national builder and you are dealing with a regional employee, a division manager, or a land acquisition manager. **You become**

a partner that helps them make a bonus because you bring opportunities to help them meet their goals.

Be aggressive.

Again, words matter. Instead of asking, "Would you mind sharing your annual goals with me?" ask, "What are your annual goals so I can help you achieve your objectives?" Positive, direct wording reinforces the partnership between you and your clients and instills confidence in them that you're the one they want to work with.

Remember, always maintain the missionary entrepreneur and developer mindset throughout all your communications before, during, and after the close.

Visit impactful-development.com to check out the checklists and training in my latest course so you don't make costly mistakes. And remember to read this chapter again before moving on to the next!

CHAPTER 12

Money Matters

Show Me the Money

In this section, we will briefly discuss the different ways you can find money to put into your deals.

Are you your own investor?

Do you have a pool of capital and enough confidence in this project that you're willing to put that money into it? If you answered yes, then you found the money you need. You probably will still need access to other capital at some point unless you are super wealthy.

Other People's Money (OPM)

Getting a loan at a bank is another option. With good credit and the ability to borrow money, reaching out to lenders may be a good choice. In the course, we teach you how to find the different types of lenders for development and land. This can be very arduous when you're new. High net-worth private investors are worth the effort!

You can partner with another developer.

A developer with deep pockets and lending relationships will often welcome working with another developer who needs funds for projects. They have existing relationships and need help keeping up with all their connections and getting those deals closed. You can be the one to help them solve this problem.

Networking to Wealth™

Get out there and network to find investors and interested parties. Open doors with DTFW™! It's okay to say, "I'm a real estate developer seeking capital for projects."

Dig deep and look for investor clubs. Look for real estate investment clubs and all the other investment groups. Study them and seek to understand what they're trying to accomplish and how you can solve problems for them. Get an audience for them and put your offer in front of them. (Your marketing package.)

Look for your area's Service Corps of Retired Executives (SCORE) chapters. Many don't think of going to SCORE, but it is a group of retired executives with connections. They have a Rolodex. A direct approach works here, such as you saying, "I've got this project for which I need this much capital. Here are my pro forma returns. Do you know anybody who might be interested in investing with me on a project like this, or can you give me some direction?"

Ideally, you may have pitched your marketing package to builders and have some interest at this point. Then you can say something about having pitched your offer to three builders, and they're showing an interest. Don't approach a prospective investor without showing them some potential due to meeting with builders. You met with the builders, did the debriefing, and now you're putting the money together.

Maximize the Wholesale Process™

In the typical wholesale model, you find something under market value and try to sell it for market value. This is a short-sighted approach and limits your return on investment.

Instead, you need to Maximize the Wholesale Process™. You need to answer the objections and answer the questions. Be a Control Freak™ right from the start because you can't wholesale something you don't control.

> Be a Control Freak™ right from the start because you can't wholesale something you don't control.

DTFW™ on the land—this is critical to the wholesale process. Know the land, know your prospective buyer, sell your position, sell your control. Yes, you sell your control, and if you control a property that you have exposed the value or created the value, you get a quick payday. That fuels your forward movement by providing the capital you need for the next project. This will help you when starting out with very little or no money.

Nobody ever sells anything they don't control.

Many people just have a short-sighted mindset that ownership is the only way to control. That's not true. Ownership is a form of control. An option contract is a form of control. An agreement to buy the land is a form of control. Understanding where you are in that process dictates how you sell your control.

Understanding where you are in that process dictates how you sell your control.

Get Creative

Is it an obstacle or an opportunity?

Keep your eyes open for creative ways to save money throughout your developer process. I'll show you a few examples below to get you started.

Build a relationship with the Fire Marshal.

When you see a piece of property with an old, dilapidated building, you can save yourself a lot of money while solving a problem for the local fire marshal. The local fire department always needs a good controlled burn to train their people.

I remember one time I found a property with an old, abandoned house. I spent $1500 to get an environmental report on the property and remove any potential environmental hazards before burning the place. The fire marshal arranged to use it for training and burned down the house to where nothing was left.

It would have cost me $10,000 to hire someone to demolish the house and haul off the debris. I saved all that money and earned myself a double benefit by creating goodwill with the fire marshal because we were willing to give him a free tool to train his team.

Example: Creative Solution...$400K in 42 days

CPAs are also excellent sources of networking. They know their clients who are out of money, have tax bills, and are separating assets. They learn about opportunities because they do the tax returns, business returns, etc.

One day, I had a CPA call me. He had a client with this old restaurant down on the waterfront. They wanted to sell or close the business, but it was an old restaurant grandfathered into a zone where this type of business wasn't currently allowed. It was continually operational and allowed to stay as long as it remained in operation. The CPA knew I could be trusted to get results while being discreet to keep the sale under the radar.

The restaurant owner told us, "I can't announce I'm closing this restaurant before you buy the property because if something happens, my income stream is gone." We let her know we could do that.

We arranged for the surveyors to go out very early and not place any flags so no one would know. We carved the land into three lots. In this case, we didn't have to do any rezonings or no public hearings. We closed, she announced the sale, and we recorded the subdivision (3 lots) the morning we closed. Everything was concurrent.

I had already sold the lots to a builder who loved building on the waterway. We owned the property for a grand total of 42 days without having to pitch a stone, lift a shovel, or pay anyone to do anything with the property at all. The builder took care of everything, even demolishing the old restaurant in exchange for some credit. We made $400,000 in 42 days on that deal.

We provided a solution for a business owner who wanted to retire while also helping solve a housing problem. In addition, we gave the restaurant owner two weeks of free rent after closing. The media showed up, and all her old customers came back to give her the best two weeks of sales in the restaurant's history. She had tears in her eyes when we sat in the restaurant after the final day. "Thank you, guys. I went out on top, and I saw people I haven't seen in years."

Value creation didn't stop there with this deal. People could come in for one last goodbye meal, and she was able to exit that business with her chin held high. It was already a win-win-win all around, but the county owned parkland next to it, and the builder ended up selling it to the county to expand the park! Now it's part of a park on the water.

Value creation doesn't always come from physically doing things. It comes from knowing things, seeing things, driving around, networking, and building up that business reputation. This is not a get-rich-quick scheme.

Get creative by understanding zoning.

If you DTFW™ and understand the UDO, a lot of creativity can come out of value creation under nuanced zoning regulations.

Turn obstacles into opportunities.

For instance, let's say you found a tract of land without water or sewer and can't do septic tanks. Without understanding zoning, you may just move on to the next opportunity. But if you read the zoning ordinance, you may see that a cemetery wouldn't need water or sewer. Now, all of a sudden, because you know the location and zoning fits for adding a cemetery here, that seemingly worthless piece of land that you can get for way under market value is worth more.

Or perhaps you noticed the land is proximate to an electric substation and qualifies for solar panels. That particular electric utility is mandated by federal law to keep increasing its power generation through alternative forms, such as wind and solar. You've found a need and a use for that land no one can build on.

What else could be built on that land when you can't have sewer and water? When you DTFW™ to know the UDO, the zoning, and the proximity of this land, you can turn worthless tracts into something valuable that presents a solution the area needs. At the same time, you save yourself money by getting the land at a lower price point.

Moving Forward

Now, you're in an opportune time to make a real impact in your area. You become a voice for the builders you build relationships with, and for the families who need affordable housing. Let me show you how in the next chapter.

CHAPTER 13

Your Voice and Your Vote Count

Be Aware of What's Happening

It's extremely important that you make it a habit to learn about the regulations and laws around land development. This is another area to Be a Control Freak™ and DTFW™. Regularly paying attention here can pay off big in time saved and disruptions avoided.

I want you to look at these areas:

- ➔ National Association of Homebuilders
- ➔ Urban Land Institute
- ➔ State Chapters of Builders Associations
- ➔ Your Local Chapters of Home Builders Associations
- ➔ Local and State Politicians

Understand their PACs (Political Action Committees) and read the emails when they encourage you to write to your congressman. You write the congressman, too, and help keep things fair for everyone. You will find tidbits of useful information that will help you offer more, avoid trouble, and build your word-of-mouth outreach by standing up for the builders and homeowners in your area.

Every year, numerous regulations and proposals are announced by people who think they're trying to help drive the cost of housing down, but many of these efforts made at a state and local level drive the costs up!

For instance, here is one great example for North Carolina. North Carolina had a bill proposal to increase the energy efficiency of housing within the state, allowing homeowners to save on their electric bills.

The state chapter conducted a study that effectively made it possible to stop the legislation. The study determined that the bill would add about $22,000 in costs per home while saving the homeowner $8 a month on their electric bill. This meant adding $100 a month to the homeowner's mortgage to save $8 a month with this "energy savings." It would take approximately 105 years before the homeowner broke even.

Even though you're a developer and not a builder, your voice makes a difference to the builders and subsequent homeowners your business is designed to help. Builders have to be empowered to buy lots at a reasonable price. The higher the construction costs are, the less they can pay for the lot because they have to sell a house at market value.

It's helpful to stay up on these movements. If you're going to make this a profession, you need to vote according to your beliefs and understand the positions of your state legislators.

Be an Advocate

It's the same principle with housing. Understanding the challenges of your state are crucial to understanding how things affect your development business and the builders you partner with. For instance, if you look at California, you'll see that it's very hard to have affordable housing there. Their environmental regulations are so substantial that they add huge costs to building a house.

The proposals, notices, and regulations at the local and state levels will often impact the ability to build on the lots you are developing. In turn, this will impact your ROI and your ability to maximize the value of your lots.

If you make this a profession, you want to create wealth and provide affordable housing as a real estate developer. You want to be impactful. That goes hand-in-hand with looking at your state chapters and getting involved.

Helpful Resources to Get You Started

You can find the National Association of Home Builders at https://www.nahb.org/

- On their Get Involved page, you can find out ways to get involved in the political process. This page contains useful links, upcoming dates of conferences, and news. You can also sign up for their monthly updates and read their BUILD-PAC.

- The Housing Economics pages help you understand data, financial outlooks, and more that affect the housing market.
- Under Press Room, you'll find news that may affect your ROI and what works best on your lots.

Suggested Press Release to Read at NAHB: NAHB Announces a 10-Point Plan to Tame Shelter Inflation, Ease the Housing Affordability Crisis

"With a nationwide shortage of roughly 1.5 million housing units that is making it increasingly difficult for American families to afford to purchase or rent a home, the National Association of Home Builders (NAHB) today unveiled a 10-point housing plan designed to tame shelter inflation and ease the housing affordability crisis by removing barriers that hinder the construction of new homes and apartments."[14]

You can find the Urban Land Institute at https://uli.org/

→ This association provides multiple resources and a real estate forum for its members. Members include real estate and land use experts. You can access regional and national product councils if you choose a full membership.

[14] National Association of Home Builders. (2024, May 1). *Nahb announces a 10-point plan to tame shelter inflation, ease the housing affordability crisis*. NAHB. https://www.nahb.org/news-and-economics/press-releases/2024/05/nahb-announces-a-10-point-plan-to-tame-shelter-inflation-ease-the-housing-affordability-crisis

Associated Builders and Contractors has a page to help you find your regional or local chapter at https://www.abc.org/chapter-locator

- → On their Get Engaged page, you can subscribe to ABC news releases for the latest economic, legal, regulatory, and industry news.

Useful Resource: State of Residential Construction Industry Report for 2024

https://go.associationofprofessionalbuilders.com/sorci-download

For more resources, visit my resource page at impactful-development.com

CHAPTER 14

Don't Mess It Up

Follow the Process

Trust and follow the process. It works. That's why we spend a lot of time within the coursework that will show you what order to check things and the priorities you must check.

For instance, if you don't follow the process, you are more than likely going to miss something that will cost you later. Here is an example from when I missed a step in the process.

I went under contract for 50 acres of land that I was excited to control. I went through the land planning, put up some non-refundable money, and blazed through the process. The problem is I missed getting a hydrant flow test to see what the water pressures were in that area until well after I spent a ton of money on this project.

This land was at the end of a county line, which is a huge red flag. When a property is at the end of a county line, that's frequently the end of the waterline. The water lines don't loop, and they lose pressure.

In this case, it meant that there wasn't enough pressure at the end of the line to serve a community or the fire hydrants required by the fire marshal. The PSI (Pressure per Square Inch) wouldn't be high enough to do any development.

I had dumped money into this 50 acres of land to get it into my control. I did the surveys and soil analysis for septic and land planning and everything else on my list but missed getting the hydrant flow test. The homes on this property would have had water dripping from their faucets and showers. If a fire occurred, they wouldn't be able to fight it.

I had to terminate the contract, give up the non-refundable deposit, eat all the expenses I incurred, and move on. **Trust the process. Missing any steps could cost you big time.**

If you want to do this business, it's critical that you take that next step. Check out my course at impactful-development.com with all the checklists. Get the coaching available to you with that course to prevent you from making these kinds of mistakes and others.

DTFW™

Don't take shortcuts, be thorough—Be a Control Freak™. **Details matter in this business.** Make sure you do all the research, read the UDO, know your market, know your builders, and build the relationships. Everything we discuss in this book will set you apart.

One common way people self-sabotage their success in this business is by freezing or fleeing when there are red flags on the property. Stay in the fight mode for something you believe in. That doesn't mean you should barrel through red flags about a property.

> Red flags on the property do not mean there are red flags in the process. Trust the process.

Fall back on the security of DTFW™ and get into the process. Do not let property red flags deter you from the process. It's common to look at ten deals before finding one to buy. You have got to work at it—the right deals don't just fall into your lap. You will have days that it feels as if they do. Then, you will have days when you wonder if you can ever find a tract of land worth anything again.

It's all about holding steady and trusting in the process. Adopt the mindset of "I'm going to make this business work, period." You can't ignore the red flags on the property. Not every property is going to work, but the process will. Believe 100% that you can become a millionaire real estate developer, but also believe 100% that red flags on a property are not an obstacle. The obstacle is not finding the problem when you should and finding it out when it becomes costly. Trust the process to find the issues with the property while 100% believing in the process and your individual worth and ability to do this.

Trust the process to find the issues with the property while 100% believing in the process and your individual worth and ability to do this.

Be a Missionary, Not a Mercenary

Your mindset matters here, and that will dictate how successful you will be at this business. Go back to Chapter Three and adopt the Missionary Entrepreneur mindset.

You are building a business with a legal and national impact, not seeking fleeting short-term gains. You are building long-term relationships that allow you to accomplish goals that positively impact the community and help change lives.

CHAPTER 15

Change Your Life While Changing Other Lives

Impact the Mission

Remember the "why" you're so engaged and enthusiastic about creating these developments that your communities want and need. My biggest "why" is to fill the gap created by the lack of housing, more specifically, affordable and workforce housing. There is a strong chance if you're reading this book, it's yours, too.

Why is it so important that you impact affordable housing?

You have a passion and understanding of the power of homeownership and you understand the positive impact it makes at an individual level. You're not just building a house: this is someone's home. You are establishing connections with builders who do not just build houses but love to allow people to live in a home and support their families.

Homes are where kids run downstairs at holiday times to open presents. It is a place where little Julia crawls into her daddy's lap and falls asleep while watching movies. A home is where children feel stable and comfortable with a sense of pride. It's a stable environment where Jack and Kim feel safe starting a new family. That home is where Jim feels a sense of accomplishment at making it on his own without living in his parent's basement until he's forty.

Building a neighborhood is like setting up dominoes that fall into one another until the final one falls and flips the switch that starts a magical display. You are the first domino. No one gets to build a home until a developer decides to create a lot.

You are the first domino. No one gets to build a home until a developer decides to create a lot.

Think about yourself as a young child. If your family were homeowners, what memories did you create in that home? How did that home contribute to making you feel comfortable and safe? What holiday traditions and visits with your grandparents do you hold safe in your heart because of homeownership?

What if your parents were not homeowners? Think about the differences they may have had in their lives if they hadn't needed to always be on the move. Think of the differences you may have experienced and felt if you hadn't needed to move constantly.

That's what drives me to develop land and to show others how to make the same impact on others as I do. My grandparents were homeowners, and my parents were not. I remember the stability and comfort of my grandparents' basement and the number of holidays we spent there. My grandparents' home was a place of consistency. As a kid, I don't remember any consistency in my parents' home for holidays and traditions. I don't remember a bad day growing up because I had wonderful parents who did the best job raising us, but there wasn't a sense of stability relative to that because of a home.

As a developer, you get to fill the gaps of stability, comfort, and freedom needed in someone else's life. You can give others what they are missing because you took that step to solve a housing problem within their community. You decided to find a Good Piece Of Land™ and make it possible for that builder to build their home.

Change Your Paradigm

By following this process and creating a new pipeline for your business, you've set yourself up for the possibility of achieving financial success. You have the potential to become a Millionaire Real Estate Developer™.

You are a control freak. You are in control of the process, which puts you in control of your success. You can be as small or as big as you wish with this business.

As a developer, you are in more control than a traditional REALTOR®. There are so many things at play within the traditional REALTOR® model that you cannot control.

> Your investment is in time, energy, and study. Knowledge is your biggest return.

It's not like opening a restaurant where you're going to dump a crazy amount of money into opening a franchise. Your investment is in time, energy, and study. DTFW™ in this process is your return. Knowledge is your biggest return.

In a world where investing in business often means risking everything in your financial future and often giving up control, you have control. You can generate revenue with knowledge and understand value creation through that knowledge.

> You can generate revenue with knowledge and understand value creation through that knowledge.

What if that knowledge could bring you an extra $10,000, $50,000, $100,000+ annually? What if you had a strong pipeline that stayed filled one, two, and three years out?

Remember, you Create Your Own Inventory™ with this process.

I Want You To Live a Charged Life!

I learned from Brendan Burchard about the three types of life you live: caged, comfortable, and charged. Caged is where you let everyone else tell you how you're supposed to live. Comfortable is the most dangerous and can hurt you the most. You never grow because you avoid all the challenges in life. Charged is where the great stuff happens. It's where I want you to be.

I hope that this book can charge you up and make you say, "I'm going to go out there and go for it." Maybe you're a real estate practitioner, and you've watched developers make millions. You've probably helped some of them make money at it already. Now it's time to Be a Control Freak™ and take things to the next level.

CONCLUSION

AI Can't Replace You

This is a long-term solution to one of America's biggest problems. This is a business where we build housing for population growth and replacement of housing stock. That's 1.4 million on average for the last 20-30 years of new housing starts in our country. It's happening out there in the world, not on social media. This isn't about how many likes you can get or how many TikTok videos you make.

When you choose to read this book and take the course and coaching that follows, you're joining me in bringing a fundamental need to our country. In many municipalities, you help provide a fundamental right that people have clean, safe, and affordable housing. You are doing that so you can make money while doing good for your community at the same time.

Your New Revenue Pipeline

After you DTFW™ and have successfully added land development to your business, you've built a degree of wealth into your life that you didn't have before. You control this revenue stream through your own team with a passion for affordable housing and real estate that contributes to your community's future.

You have a substantial inventory and a strategy for long-term growth and stability. You've established connections that make you the first person they think of calling, and they've come to trust you. You no longer worry about a lawsuit that may come your way because you're a control freak who doesn't take shortcuts.

With your success as a developer, working your business is less exhausting and much more rewarding. You have more control over your time and the process, giving you a much more rewarding career, a stronger future, and a more fulfilled family life.

It's Time To Get Started

Now that you understand the opportunity for growth and impact land development offers your real estate career, the next move is yours.

My team has made mistakes you don't have to.

We lost a lot of money when a development deal went wrong. We found a tract of land we thought was perfect for townhouses and got it zoned for townhouses—townhouses that no one wanted. They were too far out of town. D.R. Horton, one of America's largest homebuilders, best explained our mistake. Townhomes should be near the town. You should be able to see the town. Don't build townhomes in the middle of nowhere just because you can get the zoning.

We made a big mistake and had to rezone for 38 single-family homes instead of 60 townhomes. We actually had put all the infrastructure in and sold those lots to a builder, all at one take. At the end of the day, we spent around two years plus multiple public hearings, zonings, engineering—all of it. We got our money back in the end but only profited a small amount.

Big mistake, right? But, again, this is why I'm writing this book, producing the course, and offering the coaching—I can help you not make the same mistakes I did. If you look at that project, I probably made less from it than when I waited tables back in college. But those are the lessons you get with this book, and they come with the checklist you'll get inside the course. You will learn to analyze and see things, good and bad.

You'll learn things you hadn't thought of before. The different types of trees and which ones help or hurt. If a tree is thriving in soils, you know there are no sewer or septic tanks. You'll learn things like planting weeping willows will help keep a soft spot in the yard from getting muddy because it sucks up moisture at a higher rate than other trees.

You need a mindset that doesn't just aim for the finish line as a goal. This business can be fun if you embrace the journey. Enjoy the grind. The value comes from DTFW™. Throughout our coursework and coaching, we teach you how to have an emotionally and financially profitable business.

Visit impactful-development.com today for your advanced training.

How would you feel in 12 months if you sat on your hands now and did nothing? How many hours will you spend following the traditional path, exhausting your mental and physical resources to stay in front of buyers? Will you regret not taking the next step during the next real estate slump because you did not build your own inventory?

READY TO DTFW™ FOR REAL?

Your Next Step: The Impactful Development Course and Resources

You made it to the end of the book. You've seen what's possible when you shift your mindset, take control, and decide to be a developer who actually builds something that matters.

Now it's time to take the next step.

The Impactful Development course was built to help you take everything you've learned and turn it into real action. Inside, you'll find the tools, systems, and strategies I use in my own business to create real results. This is where you get serious. This is where the real work begins.

Go to impactful-development.com and get access to:

- Full checklists to walk you through the DTFW process
- Site plan and marketing package templates
- Contract examples and control strategies
- Builder tracking spreadsheets
- Real-world case studies and walkthroughs

- Step-by-step training to help you avoid the mistakes I made
- Access to coaching to get support while you build your first deal

If you've been waiting for a sign, this is it. The best time to build your pipeline was a year ago. The second best time is right now.

You can create your own inventory. You can be a control freak. You can build a business that brings you real income, real freedom, and real impact.

Start now. Don't wait until the next real estate slump to wish you had.

Get the course and resources now at impactful-development.com

DTFW™, Be a Control Freak™, and make a real impact.

Made in the USA
Columbia, SC
29 April 2025

5d833df1-f53a-4208-addc-4a77085ff235R01